Wordpress Security Fundamentals

Protect Your Website from Hackers and Identify WordPress Security Issues

Blake Webster

Books by Blake Webster

Wind Energy Essentials for the Homeowner: Common Questions about Wind Energy for the Home

Solar Energy Essentials for the Homeowner

How to Make Money Writing for the Internet

How to Self-Publish Your Book the CreateSpace Way

How to Start Your Online Photography Store

Greener Living Today: Forty Ways to a Greener Lifestyle

How to Start Your Online Affiliate Store: Step-by-Step Guide to Making Money Online

Environmentalists in Action: Profiles of Green Pioneers

Table of Contents

Overview

Hacking attempts on WordPress sites are on the rise.
Security and hosting companies such as Sucuri and HostGator report that they are seeing a large botnet that makes use of more than ninety thousand servers performing brute force attacks on WordPress sites, cycling different user names and passwords in order to gain access to sites that are vulnerable.

Wikipedia defines illegal botnets as follows:

Botnets sometimes compromise computers whose security defenses have been breached and control conceded to a third party. Each such compromised device, known as a "bot", is created when a computer is penetrated by software from a malware (malicious software) distribution. The controller of a botnet is able to direct the activities of these compromised computers through communication channels formed by standards-based network protocols such as IRC and Hypertext Transfer Protocol (HTTP).

According to BBC News, the WordPress platform currently powers more than sixty four million websites that are visited by more than three hundred and seventy one million people each month.

Survey website W3Techs reports around seventeen percent of the world's websites are powered by WordPress.

One thing we need to remember is that hacking is not personal. There is a sick feeling that develops when you discover that your site has been hacked, it's like being violated in some way. Hackers use software to find vulnerable sites, such as WordPress, allowing them to identify and inject whatever type of malicious code they are using to benefit their endeavor, be it a site that sells Viagra, a site that sells Romanian cigarettes, or spammers that are looking for comment backlinks.

What is Hacking?

In the 1990s the term "hacker" originally referred to a computer programmer that excelled in computer operating systems. Back then they might perform a little espionage by stealing a competitor's software code. During that time they also became experts at breaking into password protected computers, files and networks.

Today hackers are popularly defined as computer experts who devote their time attempting to breach the security of networks, web and email servers. It is common for them to use proprietary software to identify weaknesses and then exploit them.

Hackers tend to find WordPress to be easy prey, due to its extensive use of plugins, which total more than twenty five thousand. A recent study by Checkmarx found that no less than thirty percent of the top fifty WordPress plugins were determined to have one or more critical flaws. One of the benefits of being able to hack into a Word Press site is that it allows the hacker to hack into millions of websites.

Types of Hacking

There many types of hackers, all having malicious intent. Hackers are primarily attackers and not all of them have the intent to steal your data. The following is a breakdown of the different types of hackers.

White Hat
White hat hackers have the expert skills to break into systems and do real damage. In most cases this type of hacker will work for companies or organizations and test for security weaknesses and vulnerabilities in the network.

Black Hat
Cracker is another term for a black hat hacker who uses their skill unethical purposes such as stealing user names, passwords, credit card and bank information.

Grey Hat
As the name would imply, the grey hat hacker is a bit of a combination of the white and black hat hacker. They might be employed as a security administrator, but sometimes cannot resist the opportunity for accessing and stealing data.

Phreaker
A phreaker is a telecommunications hacker. An example of their type of hacking might be to manipulate the phone system in order to place free long distance phone calls.

Script Kiddy
The script kiddy hacker is not a professional. They rely on hacking programs and scripts to perform an attack.

Hacktivist
This is a hacker with political motivations, such as defacing the Home page of a website, leaving a political message.

Academic Hacker
This type of hacker is usually an employee or student at an academic institution who uses the computing equipment to write malicious programs.

Hobby Hacker
This hacker has a tendency to focus on home computing by using software without a license, unlocking Apple iPhones, etc.

You've Been Hacked
Identifying and Finding the Source

Whenever I am called in to consult on a hacking attempt, the first thing I do is look at the source code on the Home page. On WordPress sites I typically find the malicious code either in the header or the footer area.

The code may be in the form of an iframe. Iframe stands for Inline Frame. It is an HTML coding structure that allows another HTML document to be inserted into an HTML page. The file that is being pulled in through the iframe could perform a multitude of functions, such as redirecting your visitors, etc.

After inspecting the source code, I will look at the WordPress header and footer php files, looking for any unusual code. Nine times out of ten I will find the code in these files, but sometimes I will find it in the other php files of the design themes. After backing up the files, I will then delete the malicious code.

The following are few suggestions for identifying malware code in your WordPress site.

1. FTP into your server and look at the design themes php files and check the Last Modified date to see if there were recent changes that you did not make.
2. Check your plugins to see if you are making use of the Timthumb plugin. Timthumb is a very popular image thumbnail script and some versions have a vulnerability which allows hackers to install a virus in WordPress that leave back-doors, entry points, etc.
3. Do a search on Google or WordPress.org for new virus attacks.
4. There are security plugins that will conduct a virus scan on your site and identify problems that need attention.

A bit later in the book I will go into other methods of identifying and removing the virus codes.

Backing Up Your WordPress Site

Anyone who has had their WordPress site hacked will understand the importance of backing up your database and files on a regular basis.

Do not rely on your hosting company for regular backups. Hosting company backup schedules will vary. I have found that most of the companies will backup files on a daily basis and the MySql database on a weekly basis. Another thing to consider is that many of the hosting companies will charge a fee to restore your files.

When backing up your WordPress site it is also a good rule of thumb to have multiple backup versions, so you don't end up restoring a version that contains infected files.

I always backup my own sites and client sites to my hard drive, and then backup my hard drive to a backup cloud environment.

There are a few different methods of backing up your WordPress sites depending on what sort of server/hosting setup you have in place.

Database Backup

As I mentioned before, most hosting companies will backup your MySql database on a weekly basis, but it is wise to have a current backup on hand.

The following procedure is how I backup MySql databases to my hard drive.

You will need to gain access to phpMyAdmin located in the administrative area of your hosting account.

Call your hosting company's tech support if you can't locate it.

Enter in the user name and password that you used when setting up the database initially.

After you have logged in, select the database targeted for backup in the left navigation column.

In the top navigation area, click the Export Link.

Depending on the version of phpMyAdmin, there will be various download options to select. I usually accept the defaults and ask for a zipped SQL format.

Select a folder on your hard drive to save the file to and download the zip file.

To be on the safe side, I usually unzip the file and open it in a text editor to make certain the file is not corrupted.

File Backup

The MySql database contains all of the text and image data for your WordPress site, so you will need to backup the rest of your site files, all of which are located in the folder labeled wp-content. This folder contains any plugins you may have installed, uploaded images, your design themes, etc. I would recommend backing up the entire wp-content folder.

This is typically done using an FTP program such as WS FTP Pro or FileZilla.

Login into your server, and navigate to the wp-content folder. Locate a folder on your hard drive to save the backed up files to, and begin the transfer from the server to your hard drive.

WordPress Database Backup Plugins

Database backup plugins will make your life easier, as they save you the time of having to backup via phpMyAdmin. There are many database backup plugins to choose from and I will suggest a few that I have used.

WP-DB-Backup
WP-DB-Backup allows you to easily backup your core WordPress database tables. You may also backup other tables in the same database. Backup options allow you to save to the server, download to your computer, or have the backup emailed. Scheduling options include hourly, once or twice daily and weekly. I use this plugin for sites that are hosted with companies that do not offer cPanel, such as GoDaddy.

BackUpWordPress

BackUpWordPress will back up your entire site including your database and all your files on a schedule that suits you.

Its features include managing multiple schedules, email backup files, low memory for shared hosting accounts, email backup files, runs on Windows and Linux servers, and more.

WP-DBManager

WP-DBManager allows you to optimize, repair, backup and restore the database, delete the backup database, drop/empty tables and run selected queries. It also supports automatic scheduling of backing up, optimizing and repairing of database.

cPanel Backup Software

I saved the best for last.
If your hosting company offers cPanel, considered one of the most popular host management platforms, then your backup problems are solved.

This easy to use software quietly runs in the background of your PC or MAC and automatically downloads the current Cpanel backups from inside of your hosting account to your hard drive…safe and secure!

You have total control over how often and what time you want your sites to be backed up. And once Backup Smart is set, you can go about your business and forget about it.

When I say that it backs up your cPanel files, I mean ALL of the files, including all of your MySql databases. You can also define the number of backups you want archived. If you only want the three most recent backups, when the programs begins the fourth backup it will delete the oldest backup from your hard drive.

It saves all of the files in zip format, which is perfect for the restore function in cPanel. I'll explain more about restoring in the next chapter.

The full version of the software sells for $37.00 and you can learn more at the following address:
http://mediad.backup-smart.com

In addition to backing up to my hard drive, I then back up all of the content on my hard drive to a cloud based backup service called Carbonite.

I subscribe to the Home Plan for $59.99 per year for one computer, and it performs automatic backups with unlimited storage space.

Restoring Your WordPress Site

Hopefully if you are fully backed up you will never have to restore your website, but things happen, and if they do, at least you will be prepared.

I will cover the two most common scenarios for restoring your WordPress site.

Restoring Via FTP

The first step will be to create a new MySql database through your hosting account.

Every hosting company is different, but there will be a section in your administration area for adding new databases.

You will need to assign a database name, user name and password when setting up the database. After you have created the database, there will usually be a section that contains the details of your database, including the host path. Make a note of the database name, user name, password and host. We will need it later when setting up the configuration files for WordPress.

Now we need to import the data from our backed up MySql database. Log back into your phpMyAdmin and select the database in the left navigation column. Click the Import link in to top navigation. You will see an area that will allow you to select a file from your hard drive. Select the unzipped backed up MySql database, and click the Go button at the bottom of the page.

Next we will need to download the most recent version of WordPress. Since its open source, you can download the files for free.

Go to the WordPress homepage, www.wordpress.org, and click on the button labeled Download WordPress (Version Number) and save the files to your hard drive. The version changes on a regular basis.

To install WordPress:

1. Unzip the files. You should see everything you need to upload inside of a folder labeled wordpress.
2. Open the PHP file labeled, usually, wp-config.php. It may be labeled wp-config-sample.php; if so, rename it wp-config.php. This is the file that allows us to define the database settings.
3. Open the PHP file in a text editor such as Notepad.
4. Look for the following lines near the top of the file and edit them accordingly, inserting the database name, user name, password and host:

define('DB_NAME', 'your_database_name');

```
define('DB_USER', 'your_user_name');

define('DB_PASSWORD',
'your_password');

define('DB_HOST', 'localhost');
```

5. Save the file and upload all files, except for the folder labeled wp-content, into the root directory of your website.
6. Next upload your backed up folder labeled wp-content
7. After the upload is complete, call up the new domain in your web browser and follow the instructions, if any.
8. Log in to the Dashboard using your original WordPress user name and password.
9. You may see a notice saying that the database needs to be upgraded. Go ahead and approve.
10. Your site should be fully restored.

Restoring Via cPanel

Restoring via cPanel is child's play compared to restoring via FTP.

Depending on what happened to your website in forcing you to perform a restoration, you may have to add your domain back into cPanel.

Presuming the domain is set up in cPanel, you can restore everything by doing the following:

1. In the section labeled Files, click the Backups link.
2. Once inside the Backups section you will see three different upload areas labeled Restore a Home Directory Backup, Restore a MySQL Database and Restore Email Forwarders.
3. When we backed up our cpanel files using Backup Smart, the files were saved in three separate zip folders, all labeled appropriately. If a site had more than one database, you will see more than one database zip file.

Go ahead and upload all of the files and restoration is complete.

Brute Force Attacks

Brute force attacks are not quite the same as the regular hacks in that brute force attacks focus on simpler methods to gain access to a site. The attack will try user names and passwords over and over again until it gains access.

The attackers do this automatically with a computer program. As the speed of computer hardware becomes faster and faster the software is capable of doing more calculations per second. A brute force attack will more than likely start with one digit passwords before moving to two digit passwords and so on, trying all possible combinations until one works.

Another method called a dictionary attack tries words in a dictionary, or a list of common passwords. This approach can be very successful because people tend to use such weak and common passwords.

These attacks can be very successful when people have user names such as admin and passwords like 123456.

These attacks can wreak havoc on a server's performance, due to the large number of http requests (the number of times a visitor tries to visit a site) that will cause the server's memory to go through the roof.

These sorts of attacks happen to all web platforms, but since WordPress is so popular it ends up becoming a frequent target.

Change Your Login Regularly

It is recommended that you change your logins on a regular basis. You never know when hackers are trying to gain access to your WordPress site, hosting account or server.

WordPress Login

Changing your password can be done through the WordPress dashboard under Users in the left navigation column.

Changing your admin username is a little more difficult and usually done through the phpMyAdmin editor for your MySql database, as it cannot be changed in the Dashboard.

Passwords in WordPress are encrypted using MD5 Hash. If you want to change it in phpMyAdmin you will need the encrypted version of your desired password.

You can generate an encrypted password by using the following tool:
http://www.miraclesalad.com/webtools/md5.php

Another approach would be to add a new User and assign them the role of administrator, then delete the old administrator.

Recommended Plugins

All In One WP Security & Firewall

This plugin is designed and written by experts and is easy to use and understand.

It reduces security risk by checking for vulnerabilities, and by implementing and enforcing the latest recommended WordPress security practices and techniques.

- This plugin will protect against "Brute Force Login Attack" with the Login Lockdown feature. Users with a certain IP address or range will be locked out of the system for a predetermined amount of time based on the configuration settings and you can also choose to be notified via email whenever somebody gets locked out due to too many login attempts.
- As the administrator you can view a list of all locked out users which are displayed in an easily readable and navigable table which also allows you to unlock individual or bulk IP addresses at the click of a button.
- Force logout of all users after a configurable time period.
- Allows you to specify one or more IP addresses in a special whitelist. The whitelisted IP addresses will have access to your WP login page.
- And more….

This plugin also addresses User Accounts Security, Database Security, File System Security and more.

You can learn more at the following address: http://wordpress.org/plugins/all-in-one-wp-security-and-firewall/

Login Security Solution

This plugin offers a simple way to lock down login security for multisite and regular WordPress installations.

- Blocks brute force and dictionary attacks without inconveniencing legitimate users or administrators
- Monitors logins made by form submissions, XML-RPC requests and auth cookies
- If a login failure uses data matching a past failure, the plugin slows down response times. The more failures, the longer the delay. This limits attackers ability to effectively probe your site, so they'll give up and go find an easier target.
- If an account seems breached, the "user" is immediately logged out and forced to use WordPress' password reset utility. This prevents any damage from being done and verifies the user's identity. But if the user is coming in from an IP address they have used in the past, an email is sent to the user making sure it was them logging in. All without intervention by an administrator.
- And more....

You can learn more at the following address: http://wordpress.org/plugins/login-security-solution/

Hosting and FTP Login

If you have been the victim of a hacking attempt it is important that you change the user names and passwords of your hosting account and your FTP server login.

If a hacker has successfully gained access to your WordPress site, they may also now have access to your hosting account and server, allowing them to cause further damage.

Contact your hosting company to learn more about making these changes.

Upgrading WordPress

As a rule, most of the WordPress upgrades address security issues, so be sure to stay on top of upgrading. WordPress will notify you of upgrades at the top of your Dashboard.

Most of us are a bit hesitant to upgrade because some of the plugins might be affected, the site may not function properly and the design theme may be impacted.

It is very easy for a hacker to find a site that has not been updated and therefore perfect for hacking.

You might think you don't care if your site has been hacked, but bear in mind, a hacked site can lose position on search engine rankings. Google will even de-list and de-index your site because it finds malicious code on your site. Google will also post a warning on your listing indicating that your site may be dangerous to visit

One thing to remember is that WordPress.org is an open-source project and thousands of developers are continually working on the code. In order to take advantage of the expanded capabilities, you must keep all your core WordPress files up-to-date.

One more thing to remember; always perform a backup before updating WordPress or any of the plugins and themes.

Upgrading Plugins

WordPress plugin vulnerabilities are one of the most common entry points for hacking attacks.

On June 18, 2013, Checkmarx reported that a significant number of the plugins within WordPress are highly vulnerable.

At this time, any developer can submit a WordPress extension to enhance the basic platform and there are no security requirements or framework that the developer must abide by.

Checkmarx also identified ten of the fifty most popular WordPress plugins are vulnerable to web attacks such as SQL injection.

Wikipedia defines SQL injection as a code injection technique, used to attack data driven applications, in which malicious SQL statements are inserted into an entry field for execution (e.g. to dump the database contents to the attacker).

Checkmarx also noted that seven of the ten most popular WordPress ecommerce plugins contain vulnerabilities and that almost eight million vulnerable WordPress plugins have been downloaded.

If you suspect that some of your plugins are vulnerable, you can check the Secunia Advisory and Vulnerability Database:
http://secunia.com/advisories/search/?search=wordpress

Secunia creates computer security software that keeps home and business computers and networks safe from cyber-attack.

To find out if there is an upgrade to any of your installed plugins, click on the Plugins link in the left navigation column of your Dashboard.
If there is an update available, you will see a yellow filed underneath the plugin indicating that there is a new version. There will usually be a link at the end allowing you to Update Now.

As usual, remember to backup everything up before updating anything!

Comment Spam

Comment spam is a fact of life with all blogs, but especially with WordPress.

Comment spammers use software that create comments made for the sole purpose of gaining a backlink. This will in turn send traffic or backlink juice (unless the blog being spammed uses the nofollow tag) to the site of the spammer. Many of the spam comments are very explicit and are delivered with links to drug or gambling related sites. Other types are more subtle, where the spam commenter actually tries to leave a relevant message on the blog, along with a backlink to their website.

Recommendations

It is only a matter of time before comment spammers find your WordPress site.

Whenever I set up a new WordPress site, I always disable commenting.

You can do this by clicking on the Settings link in the left navigation column of your Dashboard.

Next, click on Discussion.

Under Default Article Settings disable, or uncheck the line that reads: Allow people to post comments on new articles.

Many people want their site visitors to be able to leave legitimate comments.

If you want to allow comments, you will need to constantly monitor your Dashboard and moderate the comments.

If you choose to allow comments, I would suggest installing the Akismet Comment Spam Fighter.

Akismet uses a unique algorithm combined with a community-created database to "learn" which comments are comment spam and which are legitimate.

Current versions of WordPress come with Akismet installed by default, so all you need to do is activate the plugin.

After activating the plugin you will see a notice at the top of the Plugins page saying:

Akismet is almost ready. You must enter your Akismet API key for it to work.

The notice contains a link that will take you to a setup page which contains a link for obtaining your activation key.

Askimet offers paid and free activation keys.

After you have your key, enter it in the Askimet API Key field in the WordPress setup page.

Click the update options button and you finished.

Delete Pending Comments Plugin

If you still find yourself under attack, and are receiving hundreds or thousands of comments waiting for approval, you can remove all of the comments at once using the Delete Pending Comments plugin:
http://wordpress.org/plugins/delete-pending-comments/

It is simple to use and will remove all pending comments in about one second.

As usual, remember to backup everything up before using the plugin.

Delete Unused Themes and Plugins

Leaving unused themes and plugins on the site won't impact your blog directly, but if any of those files have been subject to prior attacks, hackers will still have access to your website.

Many users love trying out all of the different WordPress themes available. Some users might have twenty or more themes in their theme library. To be on the safe side, if you aren't using them, I suggest removing them.

You can remove unused themes by Clicking on Appearance in the left navigation column of your Dashboard.

Next, click on Appearance.

This is where you can manage your themes.

Underneath each of the unused themes you will see a link labeled Delete, click it and the theme will be deleted from the server.

You can remove unused plugins by clicking on Plugins in the left navigation column of your Dashboard.

Underneath each of the plugins you will see a link labeled Deactivate. After you have deactivated the link you see a link labeled Delete, click it and the plugin will be deleted from the server.

Security Plugins

At this point WordPress security should be your primary concern and there are a large number of plugins available that will address firewalls, brute force attacks, SQL injection and more.

The following plugins are ones that I use and recommend.

All In One WP Security & Firewall

The All In One WordPress Security plugin will take your website security to a whole new level.

It reduces security risk by checking for vulnerabilities, and by implementing and enforcing the latest recommended WordPress security practices and techniques.

The All In One WP Security also uses an unprecedented security points grading system to measure how well you are protecting your site based on the security features you have activated.

The security and firewall rules are categorized into

"basic", "intermediate" and "advanced". This way you can apply the firewall rules progressively without breaking your site's functionality.

Features include:

User Accounts Security

- Detect if there is a user account which has the default "admin" username and easily change the username to a value of your choice.
- The plugin will also detect if you have any WordPress user accounts which have identical login and display names. Having account's where display name is identical to login name is bad security practice because you are making it 50% easier for hackers because they already know the login name.
- Password strength tool to allow you to create very strong passwords.

User Login Security

- Protect against "Brute Force Login Attack" with the Login Lockdown feature. Users with a certain IP address or range will be locked out of the system for a predetermined amount of time based on the configuration settings and you can also choose to be notified via email whenever somebody gets locked out due to too many login attempts.
- As the administrator you can view a list of all locked out users which are displayed in an easily readable and navigable table which also allows you to unlock individual or bulk IP addresses at the click of a button.
- Force logout of all users after a configurable time period

- Monitor/View failed login attempts which show the user's IP address, User ID/Username and Date/Time of the failed login attempt
- Monitor/View the account activity of all user accounts on your system by keeping track of the username, IP address, login date/time, and logout date/time.
- Ability to automatically lockout IP address ranges which attempt to login with an invalid username.
- Ability to see a list of all the users who are currently logged into your site.
- Allows you to specify one or more IP addresses in a special whitelist. The whitelisted IP addresses will have access to your WP login page.
- Add captcha to WordPress Login form

Database Security

- Easily the default WP prefix to a value of your choice with the click of a button.
- Schedule automatic backups and email notifications or make an instant DB backup whenever you want with one click.

File System Security

- Identify files or folders which have permission settings which are not secure and set the permissions to the recommend secure values with click of a button.
- Protect your PHP code by disabling file editing from the WordPress administration area.
- Easily view and monitor all host system logs from a single menu page and stay informed of any issues or

problems occurring on your server so you can address them quickly.

- Prevent people from accessing the readme.html, license.txt and wp-config-sample.php files of your WordPress site.

htaccess and wp-config.php File Backup and Restore

- Easily backup your original .htaccess and wp-config.php files in case you will need to use them to restore broken functionality.
- Modify the contents of the currently active .htaccess or wp-config.php files from the admin dashboard with only a few clicks

Blacklist Functionality

- Ban users by specifying IP addresses or use a wild card to specify IP ranges.
- Ban users by specifying user agents.

Firewall Functionality

This plugin allows you to easily add a lot of firewall protection to your site via htaccess file. An htaccess file is processed by your web server before any other code on your site. So these firewall rules will stop malicious script(s) before it gets a chance to reach the WordPress code on your site.

- Access control facility
- Instantly activate a selection of firewall settings ranging from basic, intermediate and advanced
- Enable the famous "5G Blacklist" Firewall rules courtesy of Perishable Press

- Forbid proxy comment posting
- Disable trace and track
- Deny bad or malicious query strings
- Protect against Cross Site Scripting (XSS) by activating the comprehensive advanced character string filter. or malicious bots who do not have a special cookie in their browser. You (the site admin) will know how to set this special cookie and be able to log into your site.
- WordPress PingBack Vulnerability Protection feature. This firewall feature allows the user to prohibit access to the xmlrpc.php file in order to protect against certain vulnerabilities in the pingback functionality. This is also helpful to block bots from constantly accessing the xmlrpc.php file and wasting your server resource.

Brute force login attack prevention

- Instantly block Brute Force Login Attacks via our special Cookie-Based Brute Force Login Prevention feature. This firewall functionality will block all login attempts from people and bots.
- Ability to add a simple math captcha to the WordPress login form to fight against brute force login attacks.

WhoIs Lookup

- Perform a WhoIs lookup of a suspicious host or IP address and get full details.

Security Scanner

- The file change detection scanner can alert you if any files have changed in your WordPress system. You can then investigate and see if that was a legitimate change or some bad code was injected.

Comment SPAM Security

- Monitor the most active IP addresses which persistently produce the most SPAM comments and instantly block them with the click of a button.
- Prevent comments from being submitted if it doesn't originate from your domain (this should reduce some SPAM bot comment posting on your site).
- Add a captcha to your wordpress comment form to add security against comment spam.

Regular updates and additions of new security features

- WordPress Security is something that evolves over time. We will be updating the All In One WP Security plugin with new security features (and fixes if required) on a regular basis so you can rest assured that your site will be on the cutting edge of security protection techniques.

Works with Most Popular WordPress Plugins

- It should work smoothly with most popular WordPress plugins.

Additional Features

- Ability to remove the WordPress Generator Meta information from the HTML source of your site.
- Ability to prevent people from accessing the readme.html, license.txt and wp-config-sample.php files
- Ability to temporarily lock down the front end of your site from general visitors while you do various backend tasks (investigate security attacks, perform site upgrades, do maintenance work etc.)

The plugin is free and can be downloaded at the following address:
http://wordpress.org/plugins/all-in-one-wp-security-and-firewall/

Wordfence Security

Wordfence Security is a free enterprise class security plugin that includes a firewall, anti-virus scanning, cellphone sign-in (two factor authentication), malicious URL scanning and live traffic including crawlers. Wordfence is the only WordPress security plugin that can verify and repair your core, theme and plugin files, even if you don't have backups.

Features include:

- Sign-in using your password and your cellphone to vastly improve login security. This is called Two Factor Authentication and is used by banks, government agencies and military world-wide for highest security authentication.
- Includes two-factor authentication, also referred to as cellphone sign-in.

- Enforce strong passwords among your administrators, publishers and users. Improve login security.
- Scans core files, themes and plugins against WordPress.org repository versions to check their integrity. Verify security of your source.
- Includes a firewall to block common security threats like fake Googlebots, malicious scans from hackers and botnets.
- Block entire malicious networks. Includes advanced IP and Domain WHOIS to report malicious IP's or networks and block entire networks using the firewall. Report security threats to network owner.
- See how files have changed. Optionally repair changed files that are security threats.
- Scans for signatures of over 44,000 known malware variants that are known security threats.
- Scans for many known backdoors that create security holes including C99, R57, RootShell, Crystal Shell, Matamu, Cybershell, W4cking, Sniper, Predator, Jackal, Phantasma, GFS, Dive, Dx and many many more.
- Continuously scans for malware and phishing URL's including all URL's on the Google Safe Browsing List in all your comments, posts and files that are security threats.
- Scans for heuristics of backdoors, trojans, suspicious code and other security issues.
- Checks the strength of all user and admin passwords to enhance login security.
- Monitor your DNS security for unauthorized DNS changes.
- Rate limit or block security threats like aggressive crawlers, scrapers and bots doing security scans for vulnerabilities in your site.

- Choose whether you want to block or throttle users and robots who break your security rules.
- Includes login security to lock out brute force hacks and to stop WordPress from revealing info that will compromise security.
- See all your traffic in real-time, including robots, humans, 404 errors, logins and logouts and who is consuming most of your content. Enhances your situational awareness of which security threats your site is facing.
- A real-time view of all traffic including automated bots that often constitute security threats that Javascript analytics packages never show you.
- Real-time traffic includes reverse DNS and city-level geolocation. Know which geographic area security threats originate from.
- Monitors disk space which is related to security because many DDoS attacks attempt to consume all disk space to create denial of service.
- Wordfence Security for multi-site also scans all posts and comments across all blogs from one admin panel.
- WordPress Multi-Site (or WordPress MU in the older parlance) compatible.
- Premium users can also block countries and schedule scans for specific times and a higher frequency.

The plugin is free and can be downloaded at the following address:
http://wordpress.org/plugins/wordfence/

OSE Firewall™ Security

OSE Firewall™ Security protects your WordPress website from attacks and hacking. The built-in Malware and Security

Scanner helps you identify any security risks, malicious codes, spam, virus, SQL injection attack, and security vulnerabilities.

Features include:

New Security Features in OSE Firewall v2.0

- Manage IPs in Firewall Setting - blacklisting, whitelisting, and monitoring IPs in the Firewall IP Management Section
- Manage Security Rulesets - you can change the security rule sets to that best fits for your website's requirements in the Firewall Security Ruleset Section, which increase the performance of antivirus and antihacking.
- Email Security Threats - choose different types of security threats alert emails to receive when there's an attack
- Variables Whitelisting functions - you can whitelist some variables in the variable whitelisting configuration page in the firewall in order to avoid false security alerts.

Enhanced Security Features: Provides an industry level firewall to block common security threats

- AntiSpam - Utilizing Blacklisting IPs in Stop Forum Spam
- AntiVirus - prevent, detect and remove malware from the website, keep website secure.
- Blacklisted IP Handling methods - Trace, Delete, Track
- Security Check: Malicious User Agent blocks hundreds of the worst bots while ensuring open-access for normal traffic

- Security Check: Detect Directory Traversal that consists in exploiting insufficient security validation / sanitization of user-supplied input file names.
- Malware Check: Virus Scanning that scans for malware and variants that are known security threats, and scans for heuristics of backdoors, trojans, suspicious code and other security issues, which is the first stgae of antivirus.
- Security Prevention: DoS Attacks where automated bots constituting flooding attacks to your website.
- Security Check: Javascript Injection for any traffic including automated bots that constitutes security threats of injecting malicious javascript into your files.
- Security Check: Direct File Inclusion for any traffic including automated bots that constitutes security threats of including files on a server through the web browser.
- Security Check: Remote File Inclusion for any traffic including automated bots that constitutes security threats of exploiting "dynamic file include" mechanisms in web applications.
- Security Check: Database SQL Injection for any traffic traffic including automated bots that constitutes security threats of attacking data driven applications, in which malicious SQL statements are inserted into an entry field for execution.
- Report security threats to defined owner or security analysts

The plugin is free and can be downloaded at the following address:
http://wordpress.org/plugins/ose-firewall/

Better WP Security

Better WP Security takes the best WordPress security features and techniques and combines them in a single plugin thereby ensuring that as many security holes as possible are patched without having to worry about conflicting features or the possibility of missing anything on your site.

Features include:

Obscure

As most WordPress attacks are a result of plugin vulnerabilities, weak passwords, and obsolete software. Better WP Security will hide the places those vulnerabilities live keeping an attacker from learning too much about your site and keeping them away from sensitive areas like login, admin, etc.

- Remove the meta "Generator" tag
- Change the urls for WordPress dashboard including login, admin, and more
- Completely turn off the ability to login for a given time period (away mode)
- Remove theme, plugin, and core update notifications from users who do not have permission to update them
- Remove Windows Live Write header information
- Remove RSD header information
- Rename "admin" account
- Change the ID on the user with ID 1
- Change the WordPress database table prefix
- Change wp-content path
- Removes login error messages

- Display a random version number to non administrative users anywhere version is used

Protect

Just hiding parts of your site is helpful but won't stop everything. After we hide sensitive areas of the sites we'll protect it by blocking users that shouldn't be there and increasing the security of passwords and other vital information.

- Scan your site to instantly tell where vulnerabilities are and fix them in seconds
- Ban troublesome bots and other hosts
- Ban troublesome user agents
- Prevent brute force attacks by banning hosts and users with too many invalid login attempts
- Strengthen server security
- Enforce strong passwords for all accounts of a configurable minimum role
- Force SSL for admin pages (on supporting servers)
- Force SSL for any page or post (on supporting servers)
- Turn off file editing from within WordPress admin area
- Detect and block numerous attacks to your filesystem and database

Detect

Should all the protection fail Better WP Security will still monitor your site and report attempts to scan it (automatically blocking suspicious users) as well as any changes to the filesystem that might indicate a compromise.

- Detect bots and other attempts to search for vulnerabilities
- Monitor filesystem for unauthorized changes

Recover

Finally, should the worst happen Better WP Security will make regular backups of your WordPress database (should you choose to do so) allowing you to get back online quickly in the event someone should compromise your site.

- Create and email database backups on a customizable schedule

Other Benefits

- Make it easier for users to log into a site by giving them login and admin URLs that make more sense to someone not accustomed to WordPress
- Detect hidden 404 errors on your site that can affect your SEO such as bad links, missing images, etc.

Compatibility

- Works on multi-site (network) and single site installations
- Works with Apache, LiteSpeed or NGINX (NGINX will require you to manually edit your virtual host configuration)
- Some features can be problematic if you don't have enough RAM to support them. All my testing servers allocate 128MB to WordPress and usually don't have any other plugins installed. I have seen issues with file check and database backups failing on servers with 64MB or less of RAM, particularly if there are many other plugins being used.

The plugin is free and can be downloaded at the following address:
http://wordpress.org/plugins/better-wp-security/

BulletProof Security

The BulletProof Security WordPress Security plugin is designed to be a fast, simple and one click security plugin to add .htaccess website security protection for your WordPress website. Activate .htaccess website security and .htaccess website under maintenance modes from within your WordPress Dashboard - no FTP required. The BulletProof Security WordPress plugin is a one click security solution that creates, copies, renames, moves or writes to the provided BulletProof Security .htaccess master files. BulletProof Security protects both your Root website folder and wp-admin folder with .htaccess website security protection, as well as providing additional website security protection.

Features include:

- Root Folder BulletProof Mode/Firewall
- wp-admin Folder BulletProof Mode/Firewall
- Built-in .htaccess File Editor & File Manager
- Built-in .htaccess Backup and Restore
- One-click .htaccess website security protection from within the WP Dashboard
- .htaccess security protection against XSS, RFI, CRLF, CSRF, Base64, Code Injection and SQL Injection.......... hacking attempts
- TimThumb Vulnerability/Exploit .htaccess security protection (Firewall)
- .htaccess Lock / Unlock (404 Read-Only)

- .htaccess AutoLock On or Off
- Security / HTTP Error Logging - Log 400, 403 and 404 Errors
- Security Log: Add / Remove User Agents/Bots to Ignore/Not Log or Allow/Log
- Security Log: Turn On / Turn Off / Delete Log
- Security Log Automation: Automatically zipped, emailed and replaced based on file size
- Automatic .htaccess file updating on BPS upgrade installation
- New .htaccess security filters automatically added during upgrade
- WP Dashboard Alerts / WP Dashboard Dismiss Notices
- Anti Comment Spam .htaccess code - works together with Akismet or other Spam plugins to keep Comment Spam at a minimum
- Anti Comment Spambot .htaccess code - Forbid Empty Referrer Spambots
- Custom Code feature: Add, Edit, Modify, Save additional Bonus or personal custom .htaccess code
- WordPress readme.html and /wp-admin/install.php protected with .htaccess security protection
- wp-config.php and bb-config.php files protected with .htaccess security protection
- php.ini and php5.ini files protected with .htaccess security protection
- WordPress database errors turned off - Verification and function insurance
- WordPress version is not displayed / not shown - WordPress version is removed
- WP Generator Meta Tag filtered - not displayed / not shown
- WP DB default admin username / account check

- System Info: PHP, MySQL, OS, Server, Memory Usage, IP, SAPI, WP Filesystem API Method, DNS, Max Upload, Zend Engine Version, Zend Guard/Optimizer, ionCube Loader, Suhosin, APC, eAccelerator, XCache, Varnish, cURL, Memcache and Memcached
- Security Status Page - Displays website security status information
- File and Folder Permission Checking - CGI / DSO - SAPI check / display
- Help & FAQ page - links to BPS Guide and other detailed Help & Info pages
- Extensive Read Me! jQuery Dialog Help buttons throughout the BulletProof Security plugin pages
- Website Developer Maintenance Mode (503 website open to Developer / Site Owner ONLY)
- Log in / out of your website while in Maintenance Mode
- Customizable 503 Website Under Maintenance page
- HUD Success / Error message display
- i18n Language Translation coding

BulletProof Security Login Security & Monitoring Features

- Brute Force Login Security Protection
- Log All User Account Logins or Log Only User Account Lockouts
- Logged DB Fields: User ID, Username, Display Name, Email, Role, Login Time, Lockout Expires, IP Address, Hostname, Request URI
- Email Alerting Options: User Account is locked out, An Administrator Logs in, An Administrator Logs in and when a User Account is locked out, Any User logs in when a User Account is locked out, Do Not Send Email Alerts

- Login Security Additional Options: Max Login Attempts, Automatic Lockout Time, Manual Lockout Time, Max DB Rows To Show, Turn On/Turn Off
- Login Security Stealth Mode: Standard WP Error Messages or Generic Error Messages.
- Login Security Stealth Mode: Enable or Disable Login Password Reset capability and links.
- Dynamic DB Form: Lock, Unlock, Delete
- Enhanced Search: Allows you to search all of the Login Security database rows/Fields

The plugin is free and can be downloaded at the following address:
http://wordpress.org/plugins/bulletproof-security/

Web Monitoring and Malware Cleanup Services

There are many web monitoring services available online today, but I am going to focus on one company, Sucuri Security.

I had two client sites that were falling under heavy attack and it was imperative that we take measures that went beyond the use of free plugins.

A colleague recommended Sucuri Security, and now I use their services for all of my clients.

Sucuri offers affordable yearly subscriptions ranging from one site plans, six-ten website plans and higher.

After subscribing, you can download and install a WordPress plugin, along with a PHP file that is uploaded to the root of your server.

The plugin and the PHP file will do the following:

- Malware & Blacklist Monitoring

- Email, SMS & Twitter Alerting
- Malware Cleanup (No page limit)
- Server-Side Scanning
- Blacklist Removal

The server side scanning will scan your site every four hours and alert you by email if it finds anything suspicious.

Occasionally I receive emails saying that Sucuri found something suspicious, but recommend that I conduct a manual check of the suspicious files. I usually know what sort of code to look for, and remove the infection.

If I receive an alert that requires cleanup, I then setup a new FTP account for Sucuri tech support, so that they can get into the server and conduct a cleanup. This typically takes a few hours.

Recently they offered a new monthly service called Web Application Firewall which is designed to function as a protective layer, CloudProxy, sitting between your website and its visitors.

There is nothing to install. You simply point your DNS to CloudProxy, and they handle the rest. They will block SQL injections, XSS, brute force attacks, and even DDOS attempts.

In addition to the security benefits, their high performance servers will speed and improve the performance of your site. That in itself is a positive aspect for SEO.

The monthly cost for CloudProxy is $9.99 and a single site yearly plan for server side scanning sells for $89.99.

Website: http://sucuri.net

Managing Multiple WordPress Sites

As a web developer, I manage hundreds of WordPress sites. Many are client sites and others are my business sites or sites that make up a private network for SEO (search engine optimization) purposes.

I needed to find a reliable way to manage all of these sites from a single control panel, so that I could address security issues by updating WordPress, plugins and themes, manage pending comments and post to multiple sites at the same time and more.

After many trials I finally found a solution that filled all of my needs and passed my reliability tests.

CMS Commander

With CMS Commander you can manage and control all your WordPress websites from a single control panel. If you own or manage multiple websites you know how tedious it can be to log into all their admin panel every day just to do some repetitive or mundane tasks – with CMS Commander that is not necessary: Do said tasks from within your CMS Commander account and apply them to all your sites at the same time with a few clicks!

At its core, CMS Commander looks very much like the admin Dashboard area of WordPress, with the difference that in CMS Commander you can do anything you would usually do on a single site of yours, on any number of your websites at the same time instead.

In addition to that CMS Commander also adds its own tools into the standard CMS tool set to enhance your productivity further and, for example, allowing you to SEO optimize all your websites, rewrite content or automatically interlink your site network for targeted keywords.

Not only is it ideal for managing client sites, but is a great tool for affiliate marketers.

CMS Commander also includes powerful affiliate content generation capabilities and autoposting features. Direct targeted content insertion into the articles you write, bulk article posting, PLR and CSV import and more can assist you in producing fresh content for your sites and help you monetize them better than ever before.

Features include:

- Post Editor: Write new posts in a powerful WYSIWYG editor with more features than the default WordPress editor, including useful tools for rewriting, content insertion and SEO optimization.
- Bulk Posting: Publish articles you are writing on any number of your websites at the same time.
- Media Uploader and Image Storage: Use the default media uploader you are used to from your

WordPress websites and store images and graphics directly in your CMS Commander account, in order to use them across all of your websites. Insert them into the posts you write in the editor as needed, at which point the image files will be transferred and saved to the website the article gets published on as well.

- 1-Click Plugin and Theme Updates: Get notified of all available updates to plugins and themes on all your websites right on the CMS Commander dashboard and install them all with a single click. Keep your whole site network up to date without any effort!

- Easy Plugin or Theme Installation: Bulk install new plugins to any number of websites simultaneously. Save a list of favorite plugins and themes in CMS Commander and install them on any new website of yours with a few simple clicks.

- Plugin management: Activate and deactivate plugins on your sites, update all plugins on all WordPress websites at the same time or install a new plugin on all your sites simultaneously.

- Theme management: Choose a new WordPress theme for all your sites, update themes on all your blogs or install a new theme to your whole network with a few simple clicks.

- Plugin and Theme storage: Upload and store all your plugin and theme .zip files in CMS Commander in order to quickly deploy them all to a new website. Installing or updating all your premium plugins becomes super easy like that!

- Automatic Backups: Automatically bulk create backups of all your WP websites at the same time. Set daily, weekly or monthly backup tasks and save the results to up to five different destinations, including Dropbox, Email and Amazon S3.

- Clone Full Websites: Completely copy a WordPress weblog from one site to another, including all data, articles, settings, plugins and themes! CMS Commander makes cloning a website a simple and straight-forward two step process.
- Article Management: View recent articles and approve or delete drafts. Edit posts directly in CMS Commander and copy them to any of your other websites.
- Bulk edit WordPress Posts and Pages: Quickly and easily change text in a large number of posts on any number of your sites, edit categories, add new tags and much more.
- Comment Management: Quickly review new comments and approve them or mark them as spam directly on your CMS Commander Dashboard, without the need to log into each of your sites.
- User Account Management: View and delete registered users and bulk create new user accounts on your sites. Bulk edit users to change their passwords, capabilities or more.
- Settings Management: Configure the settings and options of all your WordPress websites from within CMS Commander. Copy your whole configuration from one site to all the others to have your whole network stay in sync!
- Category Management: Bulk create any number of new categories on your sites, freely copy categories from one site to the others or delete unneeded ones.
- Maintenance Mode: Switch your websites into and out of maintenance mode with a single click of a button and display a custom offline message to your visitors, for example while you are working on new features or content.

- WP Robot management: Completely control the popular autoblogging plugin WP Robot from within your CMS Commander account.

Automatic Content and Monetization

In CMS Commander you can use several powerful automatic content features to enhance your websites. Automatic content in CMS Commander is not meant to replace your own unique articles but instead to enrich them, for example by easily adding related images, videos or even affiliate products that earn you income to them.

- Over 20 Diverse Content Sources: CMS Commander now supports more than twenty diverse sources providing you with related images, videos, articles, affiliate products and more from big names like Yahoo, Google, Youtube and Amazon (and the list is still growing).
- Completely Legal: All automatic content provided by CMS Commander is completely legal to be used on your own websites. Because CMS Commander only uses official API programs by the content owners themselves there can be no copyright issues.
- Enhance the Articles you are writing by inserting videos, images or more content related to your topic with only a few clicks.
- Bulk Update Your Existing Articles and insert images, videos or affiliate ads related to their titles.
- Bulk Content Posting: Need to fill a brand new site with fresh content? If so the bulk content features of CMS Commander offer you powerful tools to do so and allow you to combine diverse content from many sources, rewrite it automatically and schedule it on your websites.

- Earn More From Your Websites: 9 of the content sources in CMS Commander allow you to earn affiliate commission. Include their affiliate products in your articles to add several valuable new revenue streams to your income.
- Import PLR Articles: Import any number of text file articles and publish them, complete with support for spin tags, rewriting and adding related affiliate products to the posts.
- Import CSV Datafeeds: Easily load CSV datafeeds into CMS Commander, review or modify the imported content and then post it to any number of your websites.
- Support for Popular Rewriting Software: CMS Commander supports the powerful rewriting software TheBestSpinner, SpinChimp and SpinnerChief (all not included).

Security and Statistics

Security is our highest priority with CMS Commander for good reason. That is for example why we will never ask for any of your precious admin passwords. To use the service you only need to install a small plugin on your websites that will handle all communication through a secure and encrypted connection.

- No Need to Enter your Passwords! We will never ask for any of your passwords or website logins.
- A Secure SSL Connection handles all communication between CMS Commander and the plugin you install on your websites.
- Google Analytics Integration: Connect your Google Analytics account to CMS Commander to be able to review your website traffic stats while managing your websites.

- Network Traffic Stats: Aggregated traffic statistics of all your websites in a single graphic tell you with a single glance which of your websites are outperforming the others or which ones are having troubles.
- All Important Statistics: The stats in CMS Commander include all the most important metrics about your websites like bounce rates, the percentage of new visitors, average time on site and more.
- Custom Plugin Branding: Change the name, description and author of the CMS Commander plugin on your WordPress websites, for example to match your company branding and hide CMS Commander from your clients.
- Uptime Monitoring: We have integrated the free service Uptimerobot.com into CMS Commander to bring you free uptime statistics for all your websites right in your account. Confirm that all your sites are online or react quickly if not!

CMS Commander offers a thirty day free trial and the monthly prices accommodates budgets as low as five sites for $4.95 per month, to fifty sites for $29.90.to four hundred sites for $119.90 per month.

Setup involves installing and activating a WordPress plugin on each of the WordPress sites that you wish to manage through CMS Commander.

After loading the plugin you add your site address/URL, admin user name and password to the command center.

It also allows for creating Groups so you can categorize your sites better.

You find a full features list by visiting the following address:

http://cmscommander.com/members/aff/go?r=5400

Glossary

AdSense
AdSense is an ad serving application run by Google Inc. Website owners can enroll in this program to enable text, image, and video advertisements on their websites.

Affiliates
The publisher/salesperson in an affiliate marketing relationship.

Affiliate Marketing
An Internet-based marketing practice in which a business rewards one or more affiliates for each visitor or customer brought about by the affiliate's marketing efforts.

Application Programming Interface (API)
An interface implemented by a software program to enable interaction with other software, much in the same way that a user interface facilitates interaction between humans and computers.

Cookies
A message from a web server computer, sent to and stored by your browser on your computer. When your computer consults the originating server computer, the cookie is sent back to the server, allowing it to respond to you according to the cookie's contents. The main use for cookies is to provide customized Web pages according to a profile of your interests.

Dofollow
This is given in the HTML page of the website, in order to direct the search engines to follow that particular link to another web page or site.

FTP (File Transfer Protocol)
One of the most common methods for sending files between two computers.

FTP Server
A web server you can logon to, and download files from (or upload files to). Anonymous FTP is a method for downloading files from an FTP server without using a logon account.

HTML (Hypertext Markup Language)
HTML is the language of the web. HTML is a set of tags that are used to define the content, layout and the formatting of the web document. Web browsers use the HTML tags to define how to display the text.

Keyword
In web terms: A word used by a search engine to search for relevant web information.
In database terms: A word (or index) used to identify a database record.

Meta Description
A description tag that is intented to be a brief summary of a webpage's content.

Meta Keyword
A tag used to spotlight the keywords used in a web page.

MySQL
Free open source database software often used on the web.

Name Server
In computing, a name server (also spelled nameserver) consists of a program or computer server that implements a name-service protocol. It maps a human-recognizable identifier to a system-internal, often numeric, identification or addressing component.

Niche
A niche market is the subset of the market on which a specific product is focusing; therefore the market niche defines the specific product features aimed at satisfying specific market needs, as well as the price range, production quality and the demographics that is intended to impact.

Nofollow
Provides a way for webmasters to tell search engines "Don't follow links on this page" or "Don't follow this specific link."

Parameter
An item of information - such as a name , number, or selected option - that is passed to a program, by a user or another program.

Plug-In
An application built into another application.

RSS Feed
RSS (Really Simple Syndication) is a family of web feed formats used to publish frequently updated works - such as blog entries, news headlines, audio, and video - in a standardized format.

Search Engine
Computer program used to search and catalog (index) the millions of pages of available information on the web. Common search engines are Google Yahoo and Bing.

Search Engine Optimization (SEO)
The process of improving the volume or quality of traffic to a web site from search engines via "natural" or un-paid ("organic" or "algorithmic") search results as opposed to search engine marketing (SEM) which deals with paid inclusion.

Spam
In web terms: The action of sending multiple unwelcome messages to a newsgroup or mailing list.

Spider
A computer program that searches the Internet for web pages. Common web spiders are the one used by search engines like Google and Yahoo to index the web. Spiders are also called robots.

URL (Uniform Resource Locator)
A web address. The standard way to address web pages on the Internet (example: http://www.yahoo.com/)

About the Author

Blake Webster is a web and multimedia developer, digital product developer, web publisher, search engine optimization consultant, internet marketer, photographer, published author, environmentalist and publisher of the online magazine Greener Living Today ®.

He has taught web development and consulted businesses in the San Francisco Bay area since 1996.

He also works with authors by promoting their work online, laying out manuscripts for CreateSpace and converting manuscripts for Amazon Kindle.

In addition Blake offers workshops for WordPress, social media, social media SEO and Kindle marketing.

Learn more by visiting the following web sites:

www.mediadesignservices.com

www.socialwebmediatraining.com

www.greenerlivingtoday.com

www.ingramcontent.com/pod-product-compliance
Lightning Source LLC
Chambersburg PA
CBHW061032050326
40689CB00012B/2780